Teen Aggression & Bullying Workbook

Facilitator Reproducible Self-Assessments, Exercises & Educational Handouts

John J. Liptak, EdD
Ester A. Leutenberg

Illustrated by
Amy L. Brodsky, LISW-S

wholeperson
Stress & Wellness Publishers
Duluth, Minnesota

Whole Person
101 West 2nd St., Suite 203
Duluth MN 55802

800-247-6789

books@wholeperson.com
www.wholeperson.com

Teen Aggression & Bullying Workbook
Facilitator Reproducible Self-Assessments,
Exercises & Educational Handouts

Printed in the United States of America

10 9 8 7 6 5 4 3 2 1

Editorial Director: Carlene Sippola
Art Director: Joy Morgan Dey

Library of Congress Control Number: 2010941186
ISBN: 978-1-57025-252-5

Using This Book *(For the professional)*

Teen aggression and bullying are problems that continue to grow, often disrupting our schools, families, workplaces and communities. Causes of teen aggression and bullying vary from person to person and may include such factors as a teen having been exposed to physical or sexual abuse; violent behavior witnessed in the home or neighborhood; violence in the media; socio-economic issues such as family poverty, need deprivation, unstable family environment, lack of family support and appropriate role models; and exposure to weapons.

Teen aggression can take many forms:

- Bullying
- Fighting
- Gang violence
- Rape and molestation
- Arson
- Destruction of property
- Cruelty to animals
- Homicide
- Indirect aggression, i.e., gossiping or spreading cruel rumors
- Shooting and stabbing
- Internet and cyber-bullying

The *Teen Aggression & Bullying Workbook* is designed to help teens engage in self-reflection, examine their thoughts and feelings that lead to feelings of aggression, and learn effective tools and techniques for managing these feelings. This book combines two powerful psychological tools for the management of aggressive thoughts, feelings, and behaviors: self-assessment and journaling. Role-playing exercises are a third component to enhance empathy and allow adolescents to practice assertive bully prevention strategies.

The *Teen Aggression & Bullying Workbook* contains six separate sections that will help the participants learn more about themselves as well as how aggression impacts their lives:

Why Choose Violence? Scale helps individuals explore reasons they may act aggressively or violently toward other people.

Environmental Aggression Scale helps individuals identify the extent of their exposure to environmental violence and help them develop strategies to become more resilient.

Being Bullied? Scale helps individuals assess whether or not they are being bullied, and if so, to what extent.

Are You a Bully? Scale helps individuals identify whether they are aggressive and/or if they bully others, and to what extent.

Bystander Behavior Scale helps individuals explore how they react and respond in bullying situations.

Depression and Suicide helps individuals identify teens who may be at risk for depression and/or suicide.

(Continued on the next page)

Using This Book *(For the professional, continued)*

The Bully, the Target and the Bystander

In the *Teen Aggression & Bullying Workbook* book we refer to the following three people who make up a bullying situation: The aggressive person (the bully), the person being bullied (the target) and the people who are near the situation and watch it take place either because they just happen to be there or because they choose to be there (the bystanders).

Prior to beginning each section, you may want to use the educational handouts towards the end of the section, as a review for yourself and/or for the students.

Bullying and Special Needs Students

Throughout the years, education for students with disabilities has gone through many changes, and continues to do so. Historically, students with disabilities were educated separately from their age peers in either different classes or sent to special schools.

As public schools continue to emphasize inclusion of special needs students with disabilities into general education classrooms, educators have been mandated to focus on ways they can achieve academic success. As students with disabilities find themselves in regular classrooms with non-disabled peers, they are subject to a broad range of experiences with which they may not be able to cope. Inclusion, therefore, places special needs students at increased risk for bullying and aggression.

Facilitators need to be vigilant and proactive to protect these teens from bullying and aggression. Facilitators have an opportunity to emphasize compassion and educate the non-disabled students of the specific differences, challenges and difficulties special needs teens face daily.

Students with disabilities, especially mild disabilities, need to be involved in social skills classes and self advocacy groups/classes where they, too, learn how to speak up for themselves and share their feelings in a positive manner.

Use Name Codes for Confidentiality

Confidentiality is a term for any action that preserves the privacy of other people. Because teens completing the activities in this workbook might be asked to answer assessment items and to journal about and explore their relationships, you will need to discuss confidentiality before you begin using the materials in this workbook. Maintaining confidentiality is important as it shows respect for others and allows participants to explore their feelings without hurting anyone's feelings or fearing gossip, harm or retribution.

In order to maintain confidentiality, explain to the participants that they need to assign a name code for each person they write about as they complete the various activities in the workbook. For example, a friend named Joey who enjoys going to hockey games might be titled JLHG (Joey Loves Hockey Games) for a particular exercise. In order to protect their friends' identities, do not use people's actual names or initials – just codes.

(Continued on the next page)

Using This Book *(For the professional, continued)*

Bullying Box

Facilitators may implement a bullying box to give students a new way to report bullying incidents while remaining completely anonymous. Anonymity provides a way for students to report bullying without the fear of reprisal. Bullying boxes can be placed in many different places.

Students with disabilities need to be given explicit instruction how to use interventions such as these so that their voices can be heard.

Depression and Suicide

The Depression and Suicide eight-page section of this book is crucial for today's young people. No scales are included. A detailed questionnaire, idea-prompting lists, and relevant journal questions are designed to lead to productive in-depth discussions of how problems arise and how they can be solved.

As you utilize the handouts in this workbook, keep in mind that depression is a potentially life-threatening mood disorder that has been found to affect approximately one person in six each year. According to the American Psychological Association, approximately two-thirds of the people with depression do not even realize that they have a treatable illness and do not seek treatment. Research also indicates that about half of the people who have suicidal ideation report that they have not received care or even realized that they need help.

Given this information about depression and suicidal ideation, it is important to be aware of participants who might be at risk for depression and/or suicide. If you believe, suspect, think or know that you are working with teens who might need professional medical and/or psychiatric assistance, please support them and their families in seeking help and assistance.

The section on depression and suicide includes a variety of handouts that will help you, as well as the teen, identify those who might be at risk for depression and/or suicide.

Please preview all materials before you use them.

Teen aggression and bullying also can lead to the abuse of substances and becoming part of a cult or gang. Become aware of the warning signs for this type of behavior, and refer at-risk teens to professionals qualified to deal with these issues. The following web sites may help you in your work with aggressive teens:

> **http://www.afterschool.gov/** — Federal website for teen issues providing information about teen safety, health issues, and substance abuse.
>
> **http://www.cdc.gov/HealthyYouth/index.htm** — Information about federal efforts to stop teen aggression and school violence.
>
> **http://www.cdc.gov/ViolencePrevention/index.html** — Information about youth violence and suicide.

Layout of the Book

The *Teen Aggression & Bullying Workbook* is designed to be used either independently or as part of an integrated curriculum. You may administer one of the assessments and the journaling exercises to an individual or a group with whom you are working, or you may administer a number of the assessments over one or more days.

This Book Includes the Following Reproducible Pages in the First Five Sections:

- ❑ **Assessment Instruments** – Self-assessment inventories with scoring directions and interpretation materials. Group facilitators can choose one or more of the activities relevant to their participants.
- ❑ **Activity Handouts** – Practical questions and activities that prompt self-reflection and promote self-understanding. These questions and activities foster introspection and promote pro-social behaviors.
- ❑ **Quotations** – Quotations are used in each section to provide insight and promote reflection. Participants will be asked to select one or more of the quotations and journal about what the quotations mean to them.
- ❑ **Reflective Questions for Journaling** – Self-exploration activities and journaling exercises specific to each assessment to enhance self-discovery, learning, and healing.
- ❑ **Educational Handouts** – Handouts designed to enhance instruction can be used individually or in groups to promote a positive understanding of aggression and bullying and to provide positive reinforcement for bullies, targets and bystanders. They can be distributed, scanned and converted into masters for overheads or transparencies, projected or written on boards and/or discussed.

Who Should Use This Program?

This book has been designed as a practical tool for helping professionals, such as therapists, counselors, psychologists, teachers, group leaders, etc. Depending on the role of the professional using the *Teen Aggression and Bullying Workbook* and the specific group's needs, these sections can be used individually or combined for a more comprehensive approach.

Why Use Self-Assessments?

- Self-assessments are important in teaching various anger management skills because they help participants to engage in these ways:
- Become aware of the primary motivators that guide their behavior
- Explore and learn to "let go" of troublesome habits and behavioral patterns learned in childhood
- Explore the effects of unconscious childhood messages
- Gain insight and "a wake-up call" for behavioral change
- Focus their thinking on behavioral goals for change
- Uncover resources they possess that can help them to cope better with problems and difficulties
- Explore their personal characteristics without judgment
- Be fully aware of their strengths and weaknesses

Because the assessments are presented in a straightforward and easy-to-use format, individuals can self-administer, score and interpret each assessment at their own pace.

About the Assessments, Journaling Activities and Educational Handouts

Materials in the Assessments, Journaling Activities, and Educational Handouts sections in this book are reproducible and can be photocopied for participants' use. Assessments contained in this book focus on self-reported data and thus are similar to ones used by psychologists, counselors, therapists and career consultants. The accuracy and usefulness of the information provided is dependent on the truthful information that each participant provides. By being honest, participants help themselves to learn about unproductive and ineffective patterns in their lives, and to uncover information that might be keeping them from being as happy or as successful as they might be.

An assessment instrument can provide participants with valuable information about themselves; however, these assessments cannot measure or identify everything. The assessments' purpose is not to pigeonhole certain characteristics, but rather to allow participants to explore all of their characteristics. This book contains self-assessments, not tests. Tests measure knowledge or whether something is right or wrong. For the assessments in this book, there are no right or wrong answers. These assessments ask for personal opinions or attitudes about a topic of importance in the participant's life.

When administering the assessments in this workbook, remember that the items are generically written so that they will be applicable to a wide variety of people but will not account for every possible variable for every person. No assessments are specifically tailored to one person, so use the assessments to help participants identify negative themes in their lives and find ways to break the hold of these patterns and their effects.

Advise teen participants taking the assessments that they should not spend too much time trying to analyze the content of the questions; they should think about the questions in general and then spontaneously report how they feel about each one. Whatever the results of the assessment, encourage participants to talk about their findings and their feelings pertaining to what have they discovered about themselves. Talking about issues such as aggression and bullying can be therapeutic and beneficial.

The *Teen Aggression & Bullying Workbook* sections serve as an avenue for individual self-reflection, as well as group experiences revolving around identified topics of importance. Each assessment includes directions for easy administration, scoring and interpretation. In addition, each section includes exploratory activities, reflective journaling activities, insightful quotations and educational handouts to help participants to discover the extent of their aggressive behavior and explore their habitual, ineffective methods of managing their aggression, and to explore new ways for managing that aggression.

(Continued on the next page)

About the Assessments, Journaling Activities and Educational Handouts *(Continued)*

The art of self-reflection goes back many centuries and is rooted in many of the world's greatest spiritual and philosophical traditions. Socrates, the ancient Greek philosopher, was known to walk the streets engaging the people he met in philosophical reflection and dialogue. He felt that this type of activity was so important in life that he proclaimed, "The unexamined life is not worth living!" The unexamined life is one in which the same routine is continually repeated without ever thinking about its meaning to one's life and how this life really could be lived. However, a structured reflection and examination of beliefs, assumptions, characteristics and patterns can provide a better understanding which can lead to a more satisfying life and career. A greater level of self-understanding about important life skills is often necessary to make positive, self-directed changes in the negative patterns that keep repeating throughout life. The assessments and exercises in this book can help promote this self-understanding. Through involvement in the in-depth activities, the participant claims ownership in the development of positive patterns.

Journaling is an extremely powerful tool for enhancing self-discovery, learning, transcending traditional problems, breaking ineffective life and career habits, and helping people to heal from psychological traumas of the past. From a physical point of view, writing reduces stress and lowers muscle tension, blood pressure and heart rate levels. Psychologically, writing reduces feelings of sadness, depression and general anxiety, and leads to a greater level of life satisfaction and optimism. Behaviorally, writing leads to enhanced social skills, emotional intelligence and creativity.

By combining reflective assessment and journaling, your participants will engage in a powerful method for reducing and managing their aggressive behavior.

Thanks to the following professionals whose input in this book has been invaluable!

Amy Brodsky, LISW-S
Karen Brass, B.S.
Carol Butler, MS Ed, RN, C
Rozanne D. Cohen, B.S.
Kathy Khalsa, MAJS, OTR/L
Nirvair K. Khalsa
Sophia Korb, M.A.
Jay Leutenberg
Kathy Liptak, Ed.D.
Sandra Negley, MTRS, CTRS
Eileen Regen, M.Ed., CJE

Introduction for the Participant

It is vital to assume responsibility for your own behaviors, whether you have been bullied, or if you bully others, or if you are or have been a bystander to bullying. Frustration and confusion can lead to intimidating and jealous emotions, and these reactions are normal. When these emotions turn to aggression and bullying, they need to be managed and controlled. Aggressive behavior can take many different forms.

EXAMPLES

- **Physical Aggression** – pushing, shoving, hitting, slapping, pulling hair, kicking, vandalism, theft, physical bullying.
- **Verbal Aggression** – threatening others, intimidating others, getting others to do things they do not want to do, teasing, taunting, humiliating, name-calling.
- **Social Aggression** – gossiping about others, spreading cruel rumors, excluding others from activities.
- **Cyber Aggression** – using technology and the Internet to spread rumors about others, post negative pictures, taunt others.

The *Teen Aggression and Bullying Workbook* is designed to help you learn about your aggressive behavior toward others and others' aggressive behavior toward you.

In this book we refer to the following three people who make up a bullying situation: The aggressive person (bully), the person being bullied (the target) and the people who are near the situation and watch it take place either because they just happen to be there or because they choose to be there (the bystanders).

You will be asked to respond to assessments and exercises, and to journal about some experiences in your relationships. Everyone has the right to confidentiality, and you need to honor the right of their privacy. Think about it this way – you would not want someone writing things about you that other people could read. Your friends feel this way also.

In order to maintain the confidentiality of your friends, assign people name codes based on things you know about them. For example, a friend named Sherry who loves to wear purple might be coded as *SWP* (Sherry Wears Purple). Do not use any person's actual name when you are listing people.

Teen Aggression & Bullying Workbook
TABLE OF CONTENTS

TABLE OF CONTENTS

TABLE OF CONTENTS

TABLE OF CONTENTS

SECTION I:

Why Choose Violence? Scale

Name____

Date____________________________

Why Choose Violence? Scale Directions

Violence has become a way of life for many teenagers. They are exposed to it at home, in their neighborhood, schools, community, music, videos, television and computers. It is helpful to identify some of the reasons that teens act aggressively or violently toward other people.

This assessment contains thirty statements related to what sets off your emotions. Read each of the statements and decide whether or not the statement describes you. If the statement does describe you, circle the number in the YES column. If the statement does not describe you, circle the number in the NO column.

In the following example, the circled number under YES indicates the statement is descriptive of the person completing the inventory.

When I am aggressive toward other people it is because . . .

	YES	NO
I feel frustrated	(2)	1

This is not a test and there are no right or wrong answers. Do not spend too much time thinking about your answers. Your initial response will be the most true for you. Be sure to respond to every statement.

(Turn to the next page and begin)

Why Choose Violence? Scale

When I am aggressive toward other people it is because . . .

	YES	NO
I feel frustrated	2	1
I feel resentful	2	1
I don't have another way to let people know how I feel.	2	1
Other people are smarter than me	2	1
I do not do as well as others in sports, art, music, etc.	2	1

F – TOTAL = __________

	YES	NO
I need to show how tough I am	2	1
It's the only way to stop others from hurting me	2	1
It makes others afraid of me	2	1
I was bullied so I learned how to respond that way	2	1
It's the only way I can survive being bullied myself	2	1

S – TOTAL = __________

	YES	NO
I have grown up with that kind of behavior	2	1
Bullying happens around me	2	1
I haven't learned any other social skills	2	1
I behave this way as an outlet for my problems	2	1
I experienced inappropriate touching	2	1

EN – TOTAL = __________

(Continued on the next page)

(Why Choose violence? Scale continued)

When I am aggressive toward other people it is because . . .

	YES	NO
Other people encourage me to be aggressive	2	1
All of my friends do it	2	1
It makes me feel important	2	1
I don't have many friends and am accepted by people who are aggressive to others	2	1
It shows others that I am stronger, better and/or more important	2	1

I – TOTAL = ________

	YES	NO
I enjoy hurting or tormenting people who are different from me	2	1
They deserve it	2	1
It makes me feel like a big shot	2	1
They are weak	2	1
They should be tougher	2	1

E – TOTAL = ________

	YES	NO
I have trouble communicating what I want to say	2	1
I become angry over small things	2	1
I do not care about other people	2	1
I have difficulty knowing how to handle a tough situation	2	1
People look or act differently than my friends and I	2	1

SS – TOTAL = ________

(Go to the Scoring Directions on the next page)

Why Choose Violence? Scale Scoring Directions

The Why Choose Violence? Scale is designed to help you identify how likely you are to be aggressive and violent with other people. For the items you just completed, add the numbers in each lettered section. Put that number on the corresponding line. This will allow you to receive your individual scores. You will receive a total in the range from 5 to 10 in each section. Put that number in the space marked next to the TOTAL at the end of each section. Then, transfer those totals to the spaces below.

F - Frustration Total = ________

S - Survival Total = ________

EN - Environmental Total = ________

I - Influence Total = ________

E - Enjoyment Total = ________

SS - Social Skills Total = ________

To receive your overall Why Choose Violence? total, add together the six scores above. Total scores range from 30 to 60. Put that score in the space provided below.

Why Choose Violence? Scale Total = ________

Profile Interpretation

Individual Scale Score	Total Score for All Five Scales	Result	Indications
5 to 6	**30 – 39**	low	You do not have many aggressive thoughts or feelings in that particular area, or overall, that are causing you to exhibit violent behaviors.
7 to 8	**40 – 50**	moderate	You have some aggressive thoughts or feelings in that particular area, or overall, that are causing you to exhibit violent behaviors, but not too many to be harmful in your life and in relationships.
9 to 10	**51 – 60**	high	You have many aggressive thoughts or feelings in that particular area, or overall, that are causing you to exhibit violent behaviors.

No matter how you scored on the Why Choose Violence? Scale (Low, Moderate or High) you will benefit from doing all of the following exercises designed to help people deal with their tendencies towards violence.

Why Choose Violence? Scale Descriptions

Frustration – Teens scoring high on this scale tend to be prone to violence due to a sense of frustration in their own lives. They will lash out at others because they are unable to excel in school, sports, or other activities. They feel that violence brings them a sense of respect that they cannot achieve in other ways

Survival – Teens scoring high on this scale tend to be prone to violence in order to survive. They believe that if they are able to act tough around others, they will not be bullied themselves. They want to make others afraid of them so that violence will not be perpetrated against them.

Environmental – Teens scoring high on this scale tend to be prone to violence and are influenced by their environment (home, family, neighbors, community, friends, co-workers, etc.). They may lack appropriate role models to show them how to effectively interact with other people as a solution to problems. Some of their caregivers may be aggressive towards them, neglectful or very permissive.

Influence – Teens scoring high on this scale tend to be prone to violence due to an influence by their friends. They may be encouraged and even expected by members of their clique, groups or gangs to engage in violent behaviors. Violence helps them to feel important and to fit in with their friends.

Enjoyment – Teens scoring high on this scale tend to be prone to violence because they enjoy the sensation that it brings. They believe that other people are weak and deserve to be bullied. They see violence as a way of compensating for a lack of abilities in other areas of their lives. They enjoy being looked up to, or feared, for their violent attitude.

Social Skills – Teens scoring high on this scale tend to be prone to violence due to a lack of social skills. They may not know how to respond effectively in social situations, and they believe that certain situations are personal attacks, even though they may not be. They lack empathy and compassion for other people, and use violence as a way of solving problems.

The exercises on the next pages will help you explore your aggressive and violent behaviors and help you make changes to begin making a conscious effort to react to life situations in a better way.

Frustrating People

Your feelings of frustration can be the source of your anger and aggression toward other people. Complete the following exercise to explore the frustrating feelings you have about other people in your life. To protect the identity of the people you are referring to, use their name codes (not initials).
Example: ABC = Always Buys Cookies.

People Who Frustrate Me	What They Do to Frustrate Me	How I Could Have Thought About It
Friends (name code) *Ex: ABC*	*She's friendly with people who don't like me.*	*I don't need to be friends with everyone she is friends with. She can be friends with anyone and still be my good friend.*
Friends		
Parents / Caregivers		
Relatives		
Boyfriend / Girlfriend		
Teachers / School Personnel		
Others		

Frustrating Events

Your feelings of frustration can be the source of your anger and aggression toward other people. Complete the following exercise to explore the frustrating feelings you have about events in your life. Use your name codes.

Situations/Events That Frustrate Me	What They Do to Frustrate Me	How I Could Have Thought About It
At School *Ex: My teacher (ML)*	*He forgets that I have a learning disability and can't do the multi-steps easily or quickly.*	*I can remind him that I have a learning problem and need extra help or time to complete the assignment.*
At School		
At Home		
At Work		
With My Friends		
In the Community		
Other		

Survival

In order to survive, you may feel like you need to bully other people. Think about the people who bullied you in your life. List their name codes in the column at the left and describe how you were bullied.

Who Bullied Me	How They Bullied Me	What I Could Have Done
Ex: JMG	*Threatened to beat me up if I didn't give him my finished homework.*	*I could have asked an adult to help me with this bully.*

Environmental

Some people who are angry and aggressive live in environments in which they are exposed to anger, violence and abuse. Describe people in your environment (home, family, neighbors, community, friends, co-workers, etc.) and how they show feelings of aggression.

People in My Environment (use name code)	How They Deal with Aggression	What I Have Learned from This Experience?
Ex: BRS	*She screams at everyone.*	*There are better ways to communicate to get what I need or want.*

Influence

People who act violently often do so because they fall under the influence of the crowd they hang out with. They often have friends telling them that it's okay to bully others, and frequently urge them to do so.

My Friends (Use name code)	How They Influence Me to Be Violent or Aggressive	How I Can Think for Myself
Ex: CRG	*He tells me that my friend, who happens to be gay, doesn't deserve my friendship and tells me to be unkind to him and tease him.*	*I need to be myself, accepting people for who they are.*

Influence

How do your friends justify bullying others or getting violent with others?

What kinds of things do your friends say or do to encourage your violent behavior?

What will happen if you do not follow the crowd in being violent?

How does bullying and being violent help you to fit in with others?

How does bullying and violence make you feel?

Enjoyment

Some people seem to simply enjoy being aggressive and bullying. Complete the following exercise to explore the enjoyment that you get from hurting others. In the center column, describe how you feel when you are bullying other people.

Ways of Bullying	Feelings You Experience	Other Ways I Can Have this Feeling
Ex: Physical	*I feel powerful.*	*I can take a martial arts course.*
Physical		
Verbal		
Cyber		
Emotional		
Other		

Social Skills

Your lack of social skills can be the source of your anger and aggression toward other people. Complete the following exercise to explore how your lack of social skills frustrates you.

Where	Problems I Have	Ways I Could Behave or Communicate to Avoid Conflict
Ex: School	*Peope call me names because my skin is a different color.*	*Ignore them and make friends with people who like me for who I am. Invite some classmates over.*
At School		
At Home		
At Work		
With My Friends		
In the Community		
Other		

Ways to Manage Violence

You are able to learn to manage your violent thoughts, feelings and actions. Because they are all interrelated, a change in one factor can change your violent outbursts. Remember that this practice will take time and patience. The next time you feel a violent mood overtaking you, try the following:

1) What irrational thoughts are you thinking?

Identify the thoughts that are causing these angry feelings. For example, *"My teacher hates me and doesn't want to bother with me. I think I will key his car."* **(THOUGHTS)**

2) Identify the problem.

Take time to think about what is making you angry or upset, and then state it out loud. For example, *"I am angry with my teacher because he won't help me in class."* **(FEELINGS)**

3) Act in a calm, assertive manner.

Now think about why this may be happening and how you can ask for what you need. For example, *"Mr. Harris, would you help me after class to understand that principle a little better?"* **(ACTIONS)**

Other Ways to Manage Your Violent Outbursts

- **Exercise** – Take a walk, work out, or play some sports.
- **Listen to music** – Choose your favorite soothing or calming music that can help to change your mood.
- **Meditate** – Sit quietly by yourself and simply concentrate on your breathing. Count your breaths up to ten and then begin again. You will notice your aggressive feelings fading away.
- **Breathe deeply** – Take deep breaths and blow out very slowly. You will notice that you are becoming calmer.

Violence Quotes

In violence we forget who we are. ~ **Mary McCarthy**

Nothing good ever comes of violence. ~ **Martin Luther**

Nonviolence doesn't always work – but violence never works. ~ **Anonymous**

There are more pleasant things to do than beat up people. ~ **Mohammed Ali**

Think about the above quotations.

Choose one and write a story from your life that shows the quotation to be true.

Violence and Me

Write about what you have learned about yourself and the types of people, events and situations that push your violence-button.

How will you try to control your violent thoughts, feelings and actions?

Who can you talk with for help and support?

Causes of School and Community Violence

- Abuse, aggression and bullying
- Access to weapons
- Adults' response to bullying (angry reactions, ignoring, thoughtful questions)
- Changes in family and home life
- Community environment
- Cyber abuse
- Environmental impact (family, home, neighborhood, community)
- Gang activity
- Intolerance, teasing and hazing
- Lack of positive role models in family and greater environment
- Low income
- Media abuse
- Peer pressure
- Poor role-models and influences
- Violent games, sports, films, music, etc.

Potentially Violent Students might . . .

- have a history of violence and/or aggression
- hit, intimidate and bully
- isolate themselves from others
- abuse and kill animals
- write stories, poems or letters reflecting anger and aggression
- withdraw from others
- express anger through drawings
- appear different from others
- show little interest in school
- carry or have access to weapons
- have had a recent relationship break-up
- threaten verbally and physically
- be different than other students
- be depressed
- use illegal substances
- have family problems
- have discipline issues
- fight

SECTION II:

Environmental Aggression Scale

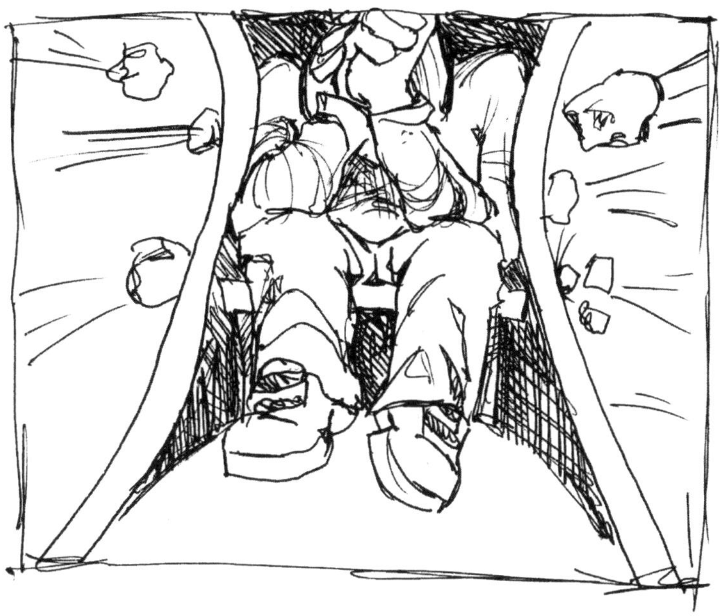

Name____

Date______________________________

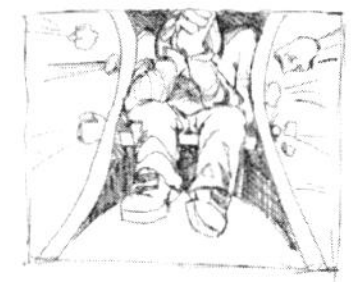

Environmental Aggression Scale Directions

Exposure to violence can have a dramatic effect on children. In fact, witnessing violence can affect teens as much as experiencing the actual violent acts. However, exposure to violence is not a determinant of future behavior. Despite this fact, many resilient people grow up to have good relationships, accept responsibility for their actions, show empathy for others and live productive lives.

The Environmental Aggression Scale can help you identify the extent of your exposure to violence on your surroundings and help you to develop strategies to become more resilient in overcoming your past.

This assessment contains thirty statements. Read each of the statements and decide if the statement is true or false. If it is true, circle the word **True** next to the statement. If the statement is false, circle the word **False** next to the statement.

In the following example, the circled False indicates that the item is false for the participant completing the Environmental Aggression Scale:

In my surroundings, the following types of violence and aggression are commonplace:

1. Destroying furniture. . . . . True (False)

This is not a test and there are no right or wrong answers. Do not spend too much time thinking about your answers. Your initial response will be the most true for you. Be sure to respond to every statement.

(Turn to the next page and begin)

Environmental Aggression Scale

In my surroundings, the following types of violence and aggression are commonplace:

1. Destroying furniture	True	False
2. Locking in rooms and closets	True	False
3. Throwing things	True	False
4. Touching inappropriately	True	False
5. Slamming doors	True	False
6. Shouting excessively	True	False
7. Intimidating physically	True	False
8. Fighting	True	False
9. Cursing	True	False
10. Beating	True	False
11. Threatening verbally	True	False
12. Withholding food	True	False
13. Insulting and hurting feelings	True	False
14. Threatening with weapons	True	False
15. Lacking positive reactions	True	False
16. Hitting	True	False

(Continued on the next page)

(Environmental Aggression Scale continued)

In my surroundings, the following types of violence and aggression are commonplace:

17. Neglecting needs . . . . True False

18. Isolating . . . . True False

19. Injuring or killing animals . . . . True False

20. Lacking communication . . . . True False

21. Abusing physically . . . . True False

22. Criticizing excessively . . . . True False

23. Ridiculing . . . . True False

24. Sexually abusing . . . . True False

25. Screaming . . . . True False

26. Name calling . . . . True False

27. Punching, kicking, choking or spitting. . . . . True False

28. Destroying property . . . . True False

29. Punishing unreasonably. . . . . True False

30. Embarrassing publicly . . . . True False

TOTAL ________________

(Go to the Scoring Directions on the next page)

Environmental Aggression Scale Scoring Directions

The Environmental Aggression Scale will to help you to identify how the violence and aggression that you have been exposed to might affect your current behavior, and guide you in developing responsible ways so you do not perpetuate those behaviors. To score this scale, add the True items you circled on the scale.

Put that number in the Total column. Then transfer it below:

Environmental Aggression Scale Total ________

Profile Interpretation

Individual Scale Score	Result	Indications
0 – 9	low	You have not been exposed to a great deal of violence and aggression in your environment. You probably have not seen or experienced a lot of fighting, shouting and physical violence growing up.
10 – 20	moderate	You have been exposed to some violence and aggression in your environment growing up.
21 – 30	high	You have been exposed to a great deal of violence and aggression in your environment. You probably saw or experienced fighting, shouting, withdrawing and physical violence growing up.

The higher your score on the Environmental Aggression Scale, the more exposure you have had to violence and aggression in your environment, and the more you must work to overcome the thoughts and feelings resulting from what you saw or experienced. No matter if you scored **Low**, **Moderate** or **High**, the exercises and activities that follow are designed to help you to explore and overcome any violence and aggression you saw or experienced.

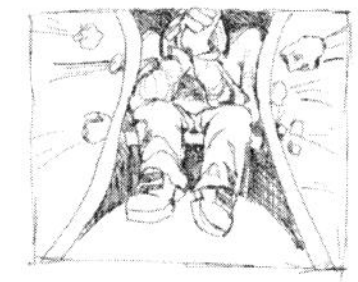

Overcoming Environmental Aggression

Resiliency

Many people grow up seeing or experiencing some level of verbal, emotional or physical aggression and violence. People who have experienced violence and aggression have succeeded despite seeing or experiencing these behaviors. They develop resiliency and the ability to overcome difficult life circumstances. They believe in themselves and the goodness of the world despite what happened in their life growing up. When people have experienced hardship in their lives, they search for ways of coping. Unfortunately, many resort to unhealthy coping skills such as drugs, alcohol and bullying. However, a variety of other means of coping that do not involve these unhealthy habits exist. The next sections will contain activities to help you to better cope with abuse, aggression and bullying you may have seen or experienced, or may be experiencing, and to help you develop your own healthy skills.

Stop Blaming

It is easy to blame others for the way you currently act. Remember that many people have experienced some aggression, and maybe even violence, in their lives. The secret is to stop blaming other people for what you have experienced or what has happened to you and begin to take responsibility for your own thoughts, feelings and actions.

People Whom You Feel are Responsible

Overcoming environmental aggression is about moving on from things that you observed or actually happened to you in your past. It is time to stop blaming the people in your surroundings for how you act. You can take control and take responsibility for your behaviors with the people you interact with on a daily basis. By taking a look at the people you feel are responsible for your current situation, you can learn to go on with your own life in a healthy, responsible way.

People in My Environment

What are some ways you can avoid some of the aggression you have been, or presently are, exposed?

School – ____

Home – ____

Neighborhood – ____________________________________

Family – ____

Friends – ____

Sporting events – ___________________________________

Other situations – __________________________________

How can you become more independent and avoid this aggression?

How can you better take control of your life despite what you have experienced?

Who can help and support you?

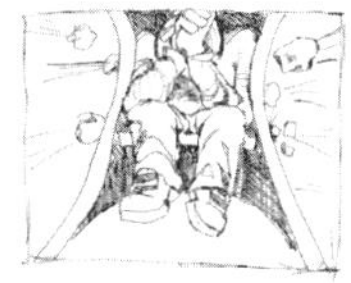

Acting Ethically

Unethical behavior is an act that violates a trust, a principle, or an accepted way of behaving. It means taking advantage of the weakness and kindness of others to make yourself feel better or for your own personal gain. In the spaces that follow, list several times when you took advantage of others to make yourself look better or to achieve some personal gain, and then list what you could have done to achieve the same result by acting more ethically. To protect the identity of the people you are referring to, use their name codes (not initials). Ex: HLP = He Likes Pizza.

People of Whom I Have Taken Advantage	What I Gained	How I Could Have Achieved the Same Result
Ex: HLP's parent	*Ride to school every day.*	*Offer to pay for gas or for my parents to share the driving.*

Choose Your Friends Wisely

Good friends are there to nurture you when you are in pain and help you make effective decisions. Do you choose friends who are positive supports and influences, or those who let you down, or engage in and encourage negative unhealthy aggressive behaviors? Think about how your relationships are affecting you both in negative and positive ways. In the spaces that follow, list your friends and identify how they affect you. Remember to use name codes when identifying your friends.

My Friends (use name code)	**How They Affect Me Negatively**	**How They Affect Me Positively**

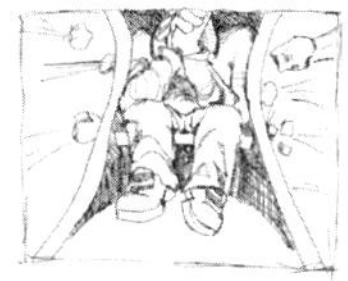

Self-Esteem

People who act aggressively often do so because they lack a positive sense of self-esteem. They believe that by belittling or hurting others, they will get attention and then feel better about themselves. This often leads to a false sense of self-esteem. You need to feel good about yourself, your strengths and accomplishments.

The Strengths I Have *Already* Developed	**Actual Accomplishments Related to These Strengths**

The Strengths I *Plan* to Develop	**Planned Accomplishments Related to These Strengths**

How I Communicate

People communicate differently in aggressive situations. Write a time below when you communicated more aggressively than usual. Use name codes.

Ways of Communicating	The Situation	How I Communicated
Body Language	*Ex: I told JFS that I was angry.*	*I had my hands on my hips.*
Body Language		
Tone of Voice		
How I Listen		
Ineffective Communications		
Statements that threaten, interrupt, or demean others		
Other		

Read your responses and think about how you feel when people communicate that way to you.

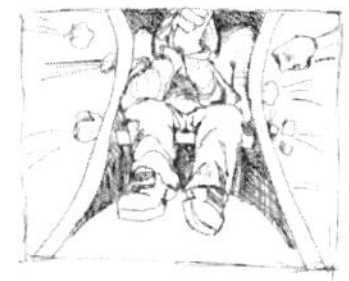

How I Reacted

Aggression is a state of being that will do you more harm than good in life. Some of the ways you can control your aggression are:

1) Recognize the thoughts that trigger your aggression and use thought-changing techniques.
2) Understand your triggers
3) Recognize body sensations that warn you of aggression
4) Use relaxation techniques.
5) Find alternatives to the problem.
6) Remember to think before you speak, act or react.

List situations when you acted aggressively, your reaction and how you could have reacted.

Aggressive Situation	How I Reacted	How I Could Have Reacted
Ex: JMB didn't catch the ball and we lost the game.	*I screamed at him and then made fun of him.*	*I could have gone over to him and said, "It could happen to anyone!"*

My Actions that I Have Blamed on Others

It is sometimes easier to blame others for your behavior. It's time to take responsibility for yourself. List the people and your action that you blame on them, how you can change that behavior and how it would change your relationship with them. Use name codes.

My Actions That I Have Blamed on Others	How I Can Change That Behavior	How Would That Improve My Relationship
Ex: JL screams at everyone, just like FLS does to me.	*I can think before I open my mouth, take a deep breath and speak in a normal voice.*	*I won't mind when JL screams at me because I'll know that it doesn't influence my behavior.*

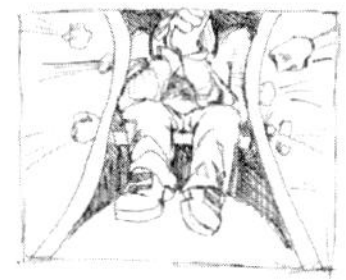

Frustration

Describe what you do when you get frustrated.

____

____

____

____

How do you calm yourself down?

____

____

____

____

Describe the type of person you are aggressive toward.

____

____

____

____

How can you be less aggressive when you get frustrated?

____

____

____

____

What can you do so you are not in so many frustrating situations?

____

____

____

____

Aggression Quotes

Everyone gets frustrated and aggressive, and I'd sooner take my aggression out on a guitar than on a person.
~ Paul Weller

Aggression only moves in one direction — it creates more aggression.
~ Margaret J. Wheatley

Journal your thoughts about either of above quotations and how it applies to you or your experiences.

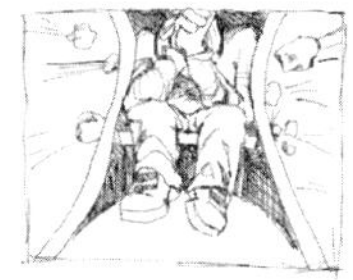

Aggressive Behaviors

Describe what you believe to be the major reasons for your aggressive behaviors.

How are you prepared to deal effectively with your aggression?

My Actions

How have your surroundings affected how aggressively you act in trigger situations?

How can you now take responsibility for not acting aggressively toward other people?

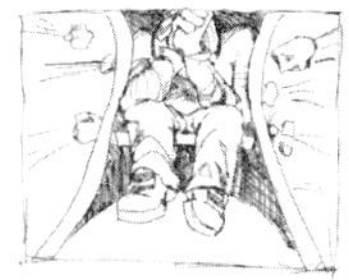

Teens are picked on because of their . . .

- physical size
- family's finances
- religion
- spiritual beliefs
- special needs and challenges
- sexual identity
- race
- ethnicity
- lack of strength
- intelligence
- abilities
- clothing
- family
- friends
- language

Teens from a violent environment may . . .

- feel fearful and anxious
- think that the world is not a safe place
- become aggressive
- be passive and withdrawn
- have trouble in school
- be likely to abuse others
- be anxious
- have difficulty connecting with other people socially and/or emotionally
- feel helpless to make changes in their lives
- have difficulty eating and sleeping
- experience anger
- become aggressive themselves
- have difficulty trusting people
- develop mental and emotional health issues
- feel depressed
- feel hopeless and helpless
- have interpersonal difficulties
- become revengeful
- have self-esteem issues
- get lower grades in school
- continue the cycle and bully others
- feel trapped

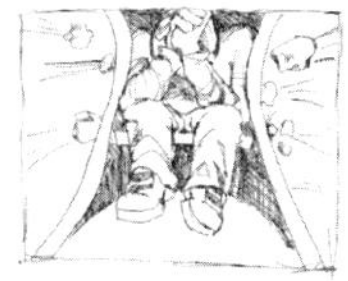

Being Exposed to Environmental Aggression

You may learn to . . .

- ask for help
- be assertive
- be less timid
- use self-defense
- empathize
- find resources available in school
- handle situations
- have more faith in yourself
- identify your true friends
- know when it's time to ask for help
- not react angrily
- run fast
- stand up for yourself
- trust your adult supports
- try new behaviors
- use a big voice

SECTION III:

Being Bullied Scale

Name____

Date______________________________

Being Bullied Scale Directions

A bully is someone who takes advantage of another individual who he or she perceives as vulnerable. It is an aggressive behavior that is intentional and involves an imbalance of power and strength. Bullying is a form of abuse that includes any behavior designed to disturb or harm another person.

Bullying takes the form of:

- physical abuse
- verbal abuse
- social abuse
- cyber abuse

Bullying can occur at home, in the schools, at a workplace and with friends, anywhere and anytime. The Being Bullied Scale will help you assess whether you are being bullied and to what extent.

This scale contains 32 statements. Read each of the statements and circle YES if the statement describes you and circle NO if the statement does not describe you.

In the following example, the circled 2 indicates that the statement OCCURS SOMETIMES for the person completing the scale.

People . . .	**NEVER**	**SOMETIMES**	**CONSTANTLY**
Push, shove, hit or spit on me	1	(2)	3

This is not a test and there are no right or wrong answers. Do not spend too much time thinking about your answers. Your initial response will likely be the most true for you. Be sure to respond to every statement.

(Turn to the next page and begin)

Being Bullied Scale

People . . .	NEVER	SOMETIMES	CONSTANTLY
push, shove, hit or spit on me	1	2	3
physically hurt me	1	2	3
kick me	1	2	3
touch me in an inappropriate way	1	2	3
take items that belong to me	1	2	3
harass or intimidate me	1	2	3
trap me in isolated places	1	2	3
damage my property	1	2	3

P TOTAL ________

People . . .	NEVER	SOMETIMES	CONSTANTLY
call me names	1	2	3
insult me or put me down	1	2	3
boss me around	1	2	3
mimic me	1	2	3
tease me	1	2	3
verbally threaten me	1	2	3
make rude comments to me	1	2	3
use words to humiliate me	1	2	3

V TOTAL ________

(Continued on the next page)

(Being Bullied Scale continued)

People . . .	NEVER	SOMETIMES	CONSTANTLY
give me the silent treatment	1	2	3
spread lies and/or rumors about me	1	2	3
find me annoying	1	2	3
purposefully leave me out of activities	1	2	3
manipulate our relationship to get something from me	1	2	3
gossip about me to other people	1	2	3
gang up on me	1	2	3
deliberately keep me out of their group	1	2	3

S TOTAL ________

People . . .	NEVER	SOMETIMES	CONSTANTLY
put up inappropriate pictures of me on blogs or websites	1	2	3
send me threatening e-mails	1	2	3
use the Internet to hurt me	1	2	3
send inappropriate text or sext messages to me or about me	1	2	3
make threatening phone calls to me	1	2	3
disclose personal data about me on websites or in chat rooms	1	2	3
post false statements about me	1	2	3
humiliate or harass me with the social media	1	2	3

C TOTAL ________

(Go to the Scoring Directions on the next page)

Being Bullied Scale Scoring Directions

There might be times when you have been bullied. This scale will help you explore the various ways you may have been bullied in your life. For each of the sections on the previous pages, count the numbers of the answers you circled for each section. Put those totals on the **TOTALS** below.

Transfer your totals to the spaces below:

P – Physical Bullying TOTAL = ________

V – Verbal Bullying TOTAL = ________

S – Social Bullying TOTAL = ________

C – Cyber Bullying TOTAL = ________

NEXT, ADD YOUR OVERALL TOTAL = ________

Profile Interpretation

Individual Scale Scores	Total Score for All Four Scales	Result	Indications
8 to 13	**32 to 53**	low	If you score low on any or all scales, you are not being bullied very much at all.
14 to 18	**54 to 74**	moderate	If you score moderate on any or all scales, you are being bullied some of the time
19 to 24	**75 to 95**	high	If you score high on any or all scales, you are being bullied a great deal of the time.

For scales which you scored in the **Moderate** or **High** range, find the descriptions on the pages that follow. Then, read the description and complete the exercises that are included. No matter how you scored, low, moderate or high, you will benefit from every one of these exercises.

In the following exercises, remember to use Name Codes for the people you describe.

Physical Bullying I

Physical bullying is physical violence or harm such as being kicked, hit, punched, pulled or touched inappropriately. Physical bullying also includes property taken from you or destroyed. In the spaces that follow, identify some of the times you have been bullied, what happened and how you reacted to the situation. Do not use names or initials, use name codes only (LTH = Likes To Hit).

Situation in Which I Was Bullied (name code)	**What Happened**	**How I Reacted**

Physical Bullying II

List a time when you were physically bullied and how. (use name code)

____

How did it feel to be physically bullied?

____

____

____

What did you do when this happened?

____

____

____

Are there ways you can avoid this type of bullying?

____

____

____

How could you have appeared to be less of a target?

____

____

____

Did you confide in anyone afterwards? If no, why didn't you? If yes, how did that work out?

____

____

____

Who are the people who could help and support you if you would contact them?

____

____

____

Verbal Bullying I

Verbal bullying includes someone who calls you bad names, teases, taunts, makes offensive remarks, criticizes you or the way you look, gossips or makes fun of you. In the spaces that follow, identify some of the times you have been verbally bullied, what happened, and how you reacted to the situation.

Situation in Which I Was Bullied (name code)	**What Happened**	**How I Reacted**

Verbal Bullying II

List a time when you were verbally bullied and how. (use name code)

How did it feel to be verbally bullied?

What did you do when this happened?

Are there ways you can avoid this type of bullying?

How could you have appeared to be less of a target?

Did you confide in anyone afterwards? If no, why didn't you? If yes, how did that work out?

Who are the people who could help and support you if you would contact them?

Social Bullying I

Social bullying is when someone excludes you from group activities, spreads rumors or stories about you, tells others something you said in private, gossips, taunts, gives you the silent treatment or makes friendship conditional. In the spaces that follow, identify some of the times you have been socially bullied, what happened, and how you reacted to the situation.

Situation in Which I Was Bullied (name code)	**What Happened**	**How I Reacted**

Social Bullying II

List a time when you were socially bullied and how. (use name code)

How did it feel to be socially bullied?

What did you do when this happened?

Are there ways you can avoid this type of bullying?

How could you have appeared to be less of a target?

Did you confide in anyone afterwards? If no, why didn't you? If yes, how did that work out?

Who are the people who could help and support you if you would contact them?

Cyber Bullying I

Cyber bullying is the use of electronic media: computers, cell phones, texting, sexting, cameras, social media, etc., to send negative messages, pictures and information to you or to other people about you. Cyber bullies don't really see it as something wrong. They think it's fun or funny and they don't see it as a big deal. They don't think they'll get caught because of technology. In the spaces that follow, identify some of the times you have been cyber bullied, what happened and how you reacted to the situation.

Situation in Which I Was Bullied (name code)	**What Happened**	**How I Reacted**

Cyber Bullying II

List a time when you were cyber bullied and how. (use name code)

____

____

____

How did it feel to be cyber bullied?

____

____

____

What did you do when this happened?

____

____

____

Are there ways you can avoid this type of bullying?

____

____

____

How could you have appeared to be less of a target?

____

____

____

Did you confide in anyone afterwards? If no, why didn't you? If yes, how did that work out?

____

____

____

Who are the people who could help and support you if you would contact them?

____

____

____

Responding to Bullies

A fact of life is that there are bullies everywhere: at school, in your community, where you work, and maybe even at home. Bullies will choose to pick on people they feel will not or cannot stand up for themselves. It is important to learn some skills that will provide you with the knowledge and confidence to assertively stand up to a bully and stop the bullying behavior. For many people, it is how they react to the bullying that determines if the bullying will continue or stop. Some techniques include the following:

ASSERTIVENESS

Assertiveness is the ability to express your feelings, opinions, and rights in a way that doesn't infringe on the feelings, opinions, and rights of other people. It means that you defend your own boundaries and those of others, but do not manipulate or threaten other people to get what you want. By learning some basic assertiveness principles, you can reduce bullying and gain respect from others.

In what situations do you find yourself not being as assertive as you should be?

When you are not acting assertively, what happens?

How does that make you feel?

(Continued on the next page)

Responding to Bullies *(Continued)*

ASSERTIVENESS *(Continued)*

Communicating assertively is the ability to express your thoughts and feelings so others know you are serious about what you are saying to them. When you feel the need to communicate assertively, remember these tips:

1) **Be aware of your body language** – Your body language often speaks as loudly as the words you use. Remain still so the bully focuses on what you are saying, not your body movements. Stand straight and tall. Try not to fold your arms across your body, because this suggests that you are defensive and unwilling to communicate assertively with the other person.

Think back to a bullying situation you were in. Describe your body language.

____

____

____

How could you have improved that body language?

____

____

____

2) **Remain calm** – This sounds difficult when you are in a bullying situation, but it is critical not to panic. Bullies can typically read how calm or how frightened you are.
3) **Provide personal space** – Maintain enough distance so that you respect the other person's personal space.
4) **Eye contact** – Maintain eye contact but try not to stare or intimidate the other person. Look into the eyes of the bully and then look slightly away for a second. This will reduce the tendency to stare down the bully.
5) **Voice** – Maintain a constant tone of voice by not to talking too fast, slow, soft or loud.
6) **State your needs** – Tell the bully what you want quickly and to the point. Talking too much will show the bully you are nervous. State what you want by using words like "I feel like . . ." and "I would appreciate if you didn't . . ." and "stop."

Practice this with a partner, taking turns, each playing the part of the bully and the victim. Explore how you feel in each of the roles.

(Continued on the next page)

Responding to Bullies *(Continued)*

IGNORING BULLIES

You can stop some verbal bullies by simply ignoring them. When doing so, remember not to show strong emotions or respond physically. The bully is trying to get you to react, but you can limit this from happening by not responding.

Practice this with a partner, taking turns, each playing the part of the bully and the victim. Explore how you feel in each of the roles.

WALK AWAY

If ignoring the bully does not work, you can also walk away. When trying this option, walk away at a normal pace, remaining tall and straight. Do not run, but be aware that the bully might continue to follow you. Try and walk to an area where you will no longer be at risk. You may need to tell the bully to "Stop!" in a calm assertive voice. When doing this maintain strong body language and eye contact.

Practice this with a partner, taking turns, each playing the part of the bully and the victim. Explore how you feel in each of the roles.

FIND HELP

If these techniques do not work, or even if they do, find the help of a supportive, trusted person.

See the next page, *Who Can I Go to for Support?* to help you figure out who those people might be.

Who Can I Go to for Support?

Sometimes, bullying happens so much that teens get used to it and start to believe that it's a normal part of everyday life. But bullying is not normal; it's not OK! It's important to remember that if you're being bullied, it is not your fault, it's the bully who has the problem. You don't have to put up with it.

When you are being bullied in any way, it is your responsibility not to be silent and to reach out for support. This would be an adult whom you can completely trust; someone you believe will help you. If you've told an adult before and that person did nothing, go to someone else. If you want someone with you to make it less scary, take a friend or brother or sister. Below, write who you can talk to about the bullying.

Who can I go to? (name code)	**Why did I choose this person?**	**If I want, who can go with me?**
Family – *Ex: Talk to and tell ASD*	*Because she's always been very understanding and honest with me.*	*My friend NGS*
Family		
Teacher		
Counselor		
Other School Administrator		
Coach		
Neighbor		
Religious/ Spiritual Leader		
Other		

Bullying Quotations

Courage is fire, and bullying is smoke. ~ **Benjamin Disraeli**

Bullying takes place in all settings. ~ **Angie Jacques**

I just want the bullying to stop. That is all I ever wanted. I used to love going to school — now I hate it. ~ **VWST – 9-year-old**

The bullying stopped when I claimed myself and proved that I wasn't afraid. ~ **Randy Harrison**

Never be bullied into silence. Never allow yourself to be made a victim. Accept no one definition of your life, but define yourself. ~ **Harvey S. Firestone**

Journal your thoughts about one of above quotations and how it applies to you.

U.S. President Barack Obama

You are not alone. You didn't do anything wrong. You didn't do anything to deserve being bullied. And there is a whole world waiting for you, filled with possibilities. There are people out there who love you and care about you just the way you are. And so, if you ever feel like because of bullying, because of what people are saying, that you're getting down on yourself, you've got to make sure to reach out to people you trust. Whether it's your parents, teachers, folks that you know care about you just the way you are. You've got to reach out to them - don't feel like you're in this by yourself.

Name one, two or three people to whom you will reach out if needed.

Ways You Can Help Yourself when Being Bullied

- Build your self-image and self-confidence
- Learn how to interact effectively with your peers and pick up on important social cues
- Develop a social support network, family, friends and trusted adults.
- Act more assertive in your interactions with potential bullies
- Use a buddy system with one friend or a group of friends
- Act brave
- Hold your anger
- Use a big, steady voice
- Display strong, confident body language
- Walk tall
- Avoid a reaction or emotion
- Don't let words upset you
- Stay calm and alert
- Take a non-violent stand.
  "I don't want to fight you." "Stop"
- Report it to the authorities
- Find safety and call for help
- Avoid being in unsupervised or unsafe areas
- Don't be mean

Bullies

- act irresponsibly
- act recklessly
- are angry inside
- are arrogant
- are average students
- are confrontational
- are hostile
- are narcissistic
- are physically strong
- are surrounded by violence
- are unconcerned about rules
- are unhappy and want to bring others down to their level
- become easily annoyed
- become easily frustrated
- behave in emotionally immature ways
- blame everyone but themselves
- count on the fact that victims won't report them
- display no compassion
- do not care about consequences
- dominate
- don't like rules
- enjoy recognition
- feel envy of others
- feel rejected
- feel resentment
- feel weak and need to show strength
- frequently fight
- get bored easily
- get excited by victims' reactions
- have little concern about other people
- have a false sense of self-esteem
- have rigid personalities
- have small networks of friends
- have inappropriate attitudes to sexual matters
- have buttons pushed easily
- have no conscience
- hide bullying behaviors
- are intolerant of racial, cultural, gender differences
- lack helpful counseling
- lack empathy
- lie
- like power
- like revenge
- like to have and be in control
- look down at anyone challenged or handicapped in any way
- mimic
- need to control
- seem innocent and nice to other people
- show a lack of anger-management skills
- think 'money talks'
- thrive on acceptance
- use people
- view violence as a positive thing
- want to appear 'cool'
- want attention from their pals and/or bystanders

SECTION IV:

Are You a Bully? Scale

Name____

Date______________________________

Are You a Bully? Scale Directions

Bullying is a form of abuse that includes any behavior designed to disturb or harm another person. It takes the form of physical abuse, verbal abuse, social abuse, and cyber abuse. Bullying can occur at home, in the schools, at a workplace, with friends — anywhere. A bully is someone who takes advantage of another individual whom she or he perceives as vulnerable. It is aggressive behavior that is intentional and involves an imbalance of power or strength. Often bullies don't view themselves as bullies. They think they're "just fooling around." The Are You a Bully? Scale is designed to identify whether you bully other people and to what extent.

This assessment contains 32 statements. Read each of the statements and circle YES if the statement describes you and circle NO if the statement does not describe you.

In the following example, the circled YES indicates that statement is **True** for the person completing the scale.

When I am with others who are weaker than me . . .

I push, shove, hit or spit . . . . YES (circled)   NO

This is not a test and there are no right or wrong answers. Do not spend too much time thinking about your answers. Your initial response will likely be the most true for you. Be sure to respond to every statement.

(Turn to the next page and begin)

Are You a Bully? Scale

When I am with others who are weaker than me . . .

I push, shove, hit or spit . . . . YES NO

I physically hurt them . . . . YES NO

I kick . . . . YES NO

I touch them in an inappropriate way . . . . YES NO

I take items that belong to them . . . . YES NO

I harass or intimidate . . . . YES NO

I trap them in isolated places . . . . YES NO

I damage their property . . . . YES NO

P TOTAL _______________

When I am with others who are weaker than me . . .

I call them names. . . . . YES NO

I insult them or put them down . . . . YES NO

I boss them around . . . . YES NO

I mimic them . . . . YES NO

I tease them . . . . YES NO

I verbally threaten them . . . . YES NO

I make rude comments to them . . . . YES NO

I use words to humiliate them . . . . YES NO

V TOTAL _______________

(Continued on the next page)

(Are You a Bully? Scale continued)

When I am with others who are weaker than me . . .

I give them the silent treatment	YES	NO
I spread lies and/or rumors about them	YES	NO
I find them annoying	YES	NO
I purposefully leave them out of activities	YES	NO
I manipulate our relationship to get something from them	YES	NO
I gossip about them to other people	YES	NO
I gang up on them with others	YES	NO
I deliberately keep them out of my group	YES	NO

S TOTAL ____________

When possible, . . .

I put up inappropriate pictures of them on blogs or websites	YES	NO
I send them threatening e-mails	YES	NO
I use my computer to hurt them	YES	NO
I send inappropriate text/sext messages to them or about them	YES	NO
I make threatening phone calls to them	YES	NO
I disclose personal data about them on websites or chat rooms	YES	NO
I post false statements about them	YES	NO
I try to humiliate or harass them on the Internet	YES	NO

C TOTAL ____________

(Go to the Scoring Directions on the next page)

Are You a Bully? Scale Scoring Directions

There are probably times when you bullied other people. This assessment will help you to explore the various ways you may have been a bully. For each of the sections on the previous pages, count the number of YES answers you circled. Put that total on the line marked TOTAL at the end of each section.

Transfer your totals to the spaces below:

P – Physical Bullying Total = ________

V – Verbal Bullying Total = ________

S – Social Bullying Total = ________

C – Cyber Bullying Total = ________

ADD YOUR OVERALL TOTAL = ________

Profile Interpretation

Individual Scale Scores	Total Score for All Four Scales	Result	Indications
6 to 8	**22 to 32**	high	If you score high on any or all scales, you tend to show a great many of the characteristics of a bully.
3 to 5	**11 to 21**	moderate	If you score moderate on any or all scales, you show some of the characteristics of a bully.
0 to 2	**0 to 10**	low	If you score low on any or all scales, you tend to show few or no characteristics of a bully.

For scales which you scored in the **Moderate** or **High** range, find the descriptions on the pages that follow. Then, read the description and complete the exercises that are included. No matter how you scored, low, moderate or high, you will benefit from every one of these exercises.

In the following exercises, remember to use Name Codes for the people you describe.

Physical Bullying

Physical bullying is threatening someone with physical violence or harms such as kicking, hitting, punching, pulling or touching inappropriately. Physical bullying also includes taking or destroying property.

Note a time when you physically bullied another person. List the person's name code and describe the situation. Do not use names or initials, use name codes only (SAM = She Annoys Me).

Name Code ____________

Situation ____

____

What did you do?

____

____

Why did you do that?

____

____

How did the person respond?

____

____

How did it make you feel?

____

____

How do you think the other person felt?

____

____

How does this add to or take away from your self-esteem?

____

____

Verbal Bullying

Verbal bullying includes calling people bad names, teasing, taunting, making offensive remarks, criticizing them or the way they look, gossiping or making fun of them.

Note a time when you verbally bullied another person. In the spaces that follow, identify some of the times you have verbally bullied, what happened, and how you reacted to the situation. List the person's name code and describe the situation.

Name Code ____________

Situation ____

____

What did you do?

____

____

Why did you do that?

____

____

How did the person respond?

____

____

How did it make you feel?

____

____

How do you think the other person felt?

____

____

How does this add or take away from your self-esteem?

____

____

Social Bullying

Social bullying is excluding others from group activities, spreading rumors or stories about them, telling others something said in private, gossiping, taunting, giving the silent treatment or making friendship conditional.

Note a time when you bullied another person. In the spaces that follow, identify some of the times you have socially bullied, what happened, and how you reacted to the situation. List the person's name code and describe the situation.

Name Code ______________

Situation ____

____

What did you do?

____

____

Why did you do that?

____

____

How did the person respond?

____

____

How did it make you feel?

____

____

How do you think the other person felt?

____

____

How does this add or take away from your self-esteem?

____

____

Cyber Bullying

Cyber bullying is the use of electronic media: computers, cell phones, texting, sexting, cameras, etc., to send negative messages, pictures and information to other people without their permission. Cyber bullies often don't recognize it as something wrong. They think it's fun or funny and they don't see it as a big deal. They don't think they'll get caught because of their knowledge of technology.

Note a time when you cyber bullied another person. In the spaces that follow, identify some of the times you have cyber bullied, what happened and how you reacted to the situation. List the person's name code and describe the situation.

Name Code ______________

Situation ____

____

What did you do?

____

____

Why did you do that?

____

____

How did the person respond?

____

____

How did it make you feel?

____

____

How do you think the other person felt?

____

____

How does this add or take away from your self-esteem?

____

____

Dealing with Your Own Feelings

Bullies often have trouble dealing with their own feelings, so they take it out on other people. If you are having trouble controlling your own emotions, you may need to learn some basic skills. Following are some suggestions for how to handle your emotions.

STEP 1 – Awareness — One of the most important things you can do is begin to notice when you are getting overly emotional and in which situation you are responding in an aggressive way. When you feel yourself getting emotional, take a minute to notice what you're feeling and what you are thinking.

Identify a time when you had an impulse to behave aggressively in the last month.
What happened?

With whom did you behave aggressively or bully in an attempt to deal with your emotions, and what did you do?

STEP 2 – Reflection — Before you take action think about what you are about to do and if you will regret it later. Remember that your thinking often drives the feelings you experience. What thoughts were going through your head?

How could you have changed or redirected the thoughts?

(Continued on the next page)

Dealing with Your Own Feelings *(Continued)*

STEP 3 – Identify Options — Ask yourself what will happen if you choose to respond a particular way. Think about the options you have for responding to the situation. How did you respond?

____

____

____

____

How could you have responded that would have yielded better results for you?

____

____

____

____

STEP 4 – Alternative Strategies — Look for ways to deal with your destructive emotions once they have begun. What are some of the things you could do to relieve these feelings? (Take a walk, exercise, listen to music, etc.)

____

____

____

____

How would these alternative strategies help you in the long run?

____

____

____

____

____

____

Why Are You Aggressive?

Peer Pressure

How do your friends pressure you to be aggressive and to bully others?

What would happen if you chose not to be aggressive and not to bully others?

What do you need to do to be more assertive with your aggressive friends when you're having second thoughts?

How does bullying improve or hurt your relationships with your friends?

(Continued on the next page)

Why Are You Aggressive? *(continued)*

Everyone does it

Why do you feel you need to follow the crowd by being aggressive and bullying others?

What will happen if you don't follow the crowd?

It's fun

What do you enjoy about bullying others?

How do you think other people feel about being bullied?

(Continued on the next page)

Why Are You Aggressive? *(continued)*

They deserve it

Why do you think some people deserve to be bullied?

Do you think you deserve to be bullied by people older and stronger than you? How is it different?

Think about the people you bully. Why do you choose these particular people? Are you jealous of them for some reason?

It makes me more popular

With what people or group does your popularity increase?

How is it worth your self-respect, and the respect others might have of you, to be aggressive?

(Continued on the next page)

Why Are You Aggressive? *(continued)*

I like the attention

How does bullying bring you attention from others?

What do you like, or dislike, about the attention?

I am bullied, so why not other people too

How does bullying others diminish your chances of being bullied?

How do you think the people you are bullying feel?

(Continued on the next page)

Why Are You Aggressive? *(continued)*

I pick on people different than me

What types of differences push your aggression button?

Why do you think you are intolerant of people different from you?

How could you view each of these people differently by putting yourself in their place?

Who Can I Go to for Help?

If you are being overly aggressive or have been bullying anyone, children, teens, adults, animals or property, you can be helped. The first step is to find someone who you can trust, one who will help guide you towards professional help. Write who you can talk to about your actions. Use name codes.

Who can I go to? (name code)	**Why did I choose this person?**
Family – *Ex: Talk to BDF*	*She will want to help me anyway she can. She might be upset but she is always there for me, no matter what.*
Family	
Teacher	
Counselor or Mental Health Professional	
Other School Administrator	
Coach	
Neighbor	
Religious / Spiritual Leader	
Other	

Bullying

As you reflect on your behavior toward others, write about why you think you have been aggressive and a bully toward other people.

What have you learned about yourself that will encourage you to be less of a bully, and to grow from the experience?

Bullying Quotations

You will never reach higher ground if you are always pushing others down.
~ **Jeffrey Benjamin**

Think about this quote and journal your thoughts about how it applies to you.

Bullies' Past History and Looking Towards the Future

Bullies have experienced some or all of the following behaviors prior to bullying:

- Harsh and often physical punishment
- Lack of praise and encouragement
- Put-downs and criticism
- Negativism rather than positivism
- Neglect
- Physical, sexual or emotional abuse
- Disinterest from caregivers
- Lack of appropriate role models

Bullies can leave their past behind them and look forward!

- Learn from past mistakes
- Break the cycle of abuse
- Develop empathy for others who are weaker
- Develop tolerance for those who are different
- Get rid of jealousy by improving own abilities and strengths
- Set an example and/or be a role model for old friends
- Find new friends who don't need to bully

SECTION V:

Bystander Behavior Scale

Name____

Date__________________________

Bystander Behavior Scale Directions

Bullying situations usually involve the aggressive person (the bully), the person being bullied (the target) and the people who are near the situation and watch it take place either because they just happen to be there, because they choose to be there, or who know about the problem and ignore it (the bystanders). Because bullying usually occurs in front of an audience, bystander behavior is critical when bullying is occurring.

Bystander behavior is how people react and respond in bullying situations. This scale is designed to help you understand the importance of your bystander behavior in bullying situations.

This assessment contains 28 statements divided into four bystander behavior styles. Read each of the statements and decide whether or not the statement describes you. If the statement does describe you, circle the YES next to that item. If the statement does not describe you, circle the NO next to that item.

In the following example, the circled NO indicates the belief statement is not descriptive of the person completing the inventory.

If I see someone getting bullied . . .

SECTION I

I do nothing . . . . YES (NO)

This is not a test. Since there are no right or wrong answers, do not spend too much time thinking about your answers. Be sure to respond to every statement. Do not worry about totaling your scores at this point. Respond to all 28 statements.

(Turn to the next page and begin)

Bystander Behavior Scale

If I see someone getting bullied . . .

SECTION I

I do nothing	YES	NO
I think it's none of my business but I stay	YES	NO
I just stay and watch	YES	NO
I remain silent and accept what is happening	YES	NO
I don't know what to do so I just stay and watch	YES	NO
I feel sorry for the target but I don't react	YES	NO
I don't see it as my problem	YES	NO

TOTAL = ___________

SECTION II

I take assertive action to help the target	YES	NO
I stick up for the target	YES	NO
I try to discourage the bully	YES	NO
I leave and go for help	YES	NO
I distract the bully	YES	NO
I defend the target	YES	NO
I help in any way I can	YES	NO

II. TOTAL = ___________

(Continued on the next page)

(Bystander Behavior Scale continued)

If I see someone getting bullied . . .

SECTION III

I go or text for help .... YES NO

I befriend the target and ask friends to do the same .... YES NO

I tell a trusted friend .... YES NO

I advise the target to report it .... YES NO

I ask everyone to side with the target .... YES NO

I report it to an adult I trust .... YES NO

I ask the target if he or she needs help .... YES NO

III. TOTAL = ____________

SECTION IV

I make comments to the bully to provoke the attack.......... YES NO

I instigate bullying .... YES NO

I side with the bully .... YES NO

I join in once the bullying has begun .... YES NO

I encourage the bully .... YES NO

I laugh and make fun of the target.......... YES NO

I cheer the bully on .... YES NO

IV. TOTAL = ____________

(Go to the Scoring Directions on the next page)

Bystander Behavior Scale Scoring Directions

This assessment is designed to measure your bystander behavior when you witness someone being bullied. For all of the sections on the previous pages, count the number of YES answers you circled in each section. Put that total on the line marked TOTAL at the end of each section.

Then, transfer your totals to the spaces below:

SECTION I — TOTAL = _______ Accept

SECTION II — TOTAL = _______ Defend

SECTION III — TOTAL = _______ Help

SECTION IV — TOTAL = _______ Hurt

Profile Interpretation

Individual Scale Scores	Result	Indications
0 to 2	high	You probably do not possess many of the characteristics of this bystander type.
3 to 4	moderate	You probably possess some of the characteristics of this bystander type.
5 to 7	low	You probably possess many of the characteristics of this bystander type.

Depending on how you respond when you witness someone being bullied can either contribute to the problem or be part of the solution. The area or areas in which you scored the highest tends to be your most preferred bystander behavior. Similarly, the area or areas in which you scored the lowest tends to be your least preferred bystander behavior. Now turn to the next page for a description of each of the four bystander behaviors measured on the assessment.

Scale Descriptions

SCALE I – Accept

An Accepting Bystander helps the bully by not doing anything to help the person being bullied. They provide the audience the bullies need and they silently accept the bullying behavior.

SCALE II – Defend

A Defending Bystander will physically intervene in the bullying behavior by assertively confronting the bully. If this is your bystander behavior, use it cautiously as it can be dangerous and even escalate the bully's aggressive behavior.

SCALE III – Help

A Helping Bystander will use their voice and get others to support the target; encourages the target to report the behavior; asks other bystanders to leave, taking the audience away; tells the bully to "STOP" and contacts a trusted adult.

SCALE IV – Hurt

A Hurting Bystander will be harmful to the target by cheering others to bully. They will instigate aggression by prodding the bully to begin, and might even join in with the bully after it has begun.

Bullying Situations

Most people have witnessed bullying from time to time. Think about the people you have seen being bullied. Identify those people (using name codes) and explore how they were targeted and how you responded.

People I Saw Being Bullied (name code)	**What the Bully Did**	**What I Did**

Helping a Situation

Now think about the people whom you have helped from being bullied in the past. Identify those people and how you stopped the target from being bullied.

People Who Were Being Bullied (name code)	**How I Helped the Target**	**How I Felt**

Ways to Help Bullied Targets

Following are some of the other ways to help targets from being bullied. Write about the ones you would like to begin using. Please remember to use Name Codes for the people.

Ways of Helping Targets	How I Will Begin Using This Method
Help target get away	
Go for help	
Urge others to stand up to the bully	
Distract the bully	
Report bullying to a trusted adult, hotline or school personnel	
Stand tall, look the bully in the eyes and say "STOP" (or some other assertive remark)	
Befriend the target later	
Other	

Supporting a Target

As a bystander, by not helping the target you are part of the problem, not the solution. It can be scary to intervene on behalf of a target being bullied, but you can help by getting help – use your voice! This would be an adult whom you can completely trust; someone who you believe will help you. If you've told an adult before and that person did nothing, go to someone else. If you want someone with you to make it less scary, take a friend or brother or sister. Below, write who you can talk to about the bullying.

Who Can I Go To? (name code)	**Why Did I Choose This Person?**	**If I Want, Who Can Go With Me?**
Family *Ex: Talk to, and tell, NHY*	*Because she is always close by when the bullying happens.*	*My friend MKP*
Family		
Teacher		
Counselor		
Other School Administrator		
Coach		
Neighbor		
Religious/Spiritual Leader		
Other		

Tattling vs. Reporting

Tattling is when you try to get someone in trouble even though they are not hurting themselves or anyone else. If you have ever tattled on anyone (sibling, neighbor, friend, school mate, etc.) write about it below.

A Time I Tattled on Someone	Reaction of Person I Talked TO	Reaction of Person I Talked ABOUT

Reporting is when you're trying to help kids out of trouble because they might get hurt, or already are. If you have ever reported on anyone (sibling, neighbor, friend, school mate, etc.) write about it below.

A Time I Reported on Someone	Reaction of Person I Reported TO	Reaction of Person I Reported ABOUT

Strategies for a Stand-upster!

- Stay calm and cool
- Do not boo, clap or scream
- Either say nothing and leave or use a big, assertive voice to the bully:

  "You are a bully!"

  "That's mean."

  "This isn't cool."

  "STOP."

  "This isn't right."

  "Cut it out."

  "You'll get suspended."
- Ask target, "Do you need help?"
- Bullies like audiences – ask everyone, including yourself, to leave.
- Report the incident immediately to a teacher, principal, hot line, police, trusted adult, bully box at the school.
- If the school doesn't have a bully box or hot line, talk with a school official and request it.
- Use a big, assertive voice to the other bystanders:

  "Let's go!"

  "Let's leave!"

  "Are you with me?"

  "Why are you all just standing here, watching?"

  "Don't laugh, that's not funny."
- Distract the audience and the bully:

  "A teacher is coming. Let's go."

  "There's a great ballgame going on."

  "Someone just called the police."

  "Mr. Smith is looking for you.
- Use your voice.

Group Practice

Form into groups of three and practice the different types of strategies above, with one another. Decide on a bullying situation. Each person takes a turn playing the part of a bully, a target and a bystander. As the bullying begins, the bystander should practice using the techniques you discussed. Then change roles until everyone has had an opportunity to be a stand-upster. Discuss your reactions in each of the roles played.

Reflecting on My Bystander Behaviors

Journal your responses to the following situations.

Write about a time you were in a bullying situation, watched and did nothing.

Write about a time you refrained from helping a target because you were afraid the bully would find out.

Write about a time you did not help a target because you didn't want to be a snitch, tattler or informer.

(Continued on the next page)

Reflecting on My Bystander Behaviors *(Continued)*

Write about a time you felt unsafe and afraid to take action.

Write about a time you did not help a target because you thought it wasn't your business.

Write about a time you felt guilty or helpless for not helping a target.

(Continued on the next page)

Reflecting on My Bystander Behaviors *(Continued)*

Write about a time you gathered the crowd together and all left the bully standing there alone with the target.

Write about a time you have been drawn into a bullying behavior because of peer pressure.

Write about a time you told a trusted person about a bullying situation that you witnessed.

(Continued on the next page)

Reflecting on My Bystander Behaviors *(Continued)*

Write about a time you made fun of a target to keep up with the crowd.

Write about a time you felt ashamed that you didn't help someone.

Write about a time, past or present, that you worried that your actions could reflect on your friends and then they were, or would be, bullied.

(Continued on the next page)

Reflecting on My Bystander Behaviors *(Continued)*

Pick 3 of your responses from the prior four pages and journal what you could and would do differently now.

1) ______________________________

2) ______________________________

3) ______________________________

Bystander Quotes

- ❑ *All people who observe bullying may not know what to do, but they feel bad. It affects all kids.* ~ **Jerry Misik**

- ❑ *The more kids are aware of what bullying is, the better. Simple teasing can really take a toll on a kid. We just want kids to know bullying when they see it, so they can at least try and stop it.*
  ~ **Carl Sousa**

- ❑ *It's getting to the students who are being bullied and those who are doing the bullying. If you can eliminate either group — if those who are being bullied can stand up for themselves, or the teasing stops — the oppression will end.*
  ~ **Sasha Neumann**

- ❑ *One of the ill effects of cruelty is that is makes the bystanders cruel.*
  ~ **Thomas Fowell Buxton**

- ❑ *There is no such thing as an innocent bystander.*
  ~ **Abbie Hoffman**

Check one of the quotations above and journal your thoughts about how it pertains to you.

Why Do People Just Watch?

- Fear of retaliation
- Shame they can't stand up for themselves
- Fear they will be seen as a snitch
- Don't believe anything would change as a result of telling of the bullying
- Believe that telling someone will make the situation worse
- Afraid the bully will bully them
- Fear they won't be believed by parents or teachers
- Are amused by the bully
- Watching makes them feel strong
- Fear their friends will be bullied

Hurtful vs. Helpful

Hurtful	**Helpful**
Urge the bully on	Discourage the bully
Laugh	Defend the victim
Prod the bully to begin	Get outside help
Cheer on the bully	Report to adults
Join in the bullying	Assertively say "STOP IT!"
Watch and do nothing	Text for help
Provide an audience	Leave and tell an adult
Silently accept the bullying	Tell others to leave
Taunt the victim	Use your voice
Side with the bully	Say "CUT IT OUT!"
Tease the victim	Ask others to confront together
Accept and look away	Distract the bully
Be aggressive with the bully	Warn bully that someone is coming

SECTION VI:

Depression and Suicide

Name____

Date___________________________

How Teens Can Help Someone Who Might Be Depressed and Can Possibly Prevent a Suicide

Depression is an illness that involves the body, mood, and thoughts. It affects the way people eat and sleep, the way people feel about themselves, and the way people think about events and people in their daily environment.

Just as we may plan regular tune-ups for our cars or schedule annual physicals, our mental health needs to be checked as well. The stigma often associated with depressive illnesses can prevent people from asking for help.

For those of you who know someone who might be depressed or suicidal, helping this person accept and find help is extremely important. Being willing to talk about depression and suicidal thoughts with a friend, family member, or someone they know, even if it is uncomfortable or scary, could be a first step in that person's receiving help and possibly in preventing a suicide. It is important for you to use your voice!

If you recognize yourself in the following handouts, reach out and talk with a trusted adult who can assist you in finding help.

Remember, suicide permanently ends a life because of a temporary problem.

- If a friend or acquaintance tells you about suicidal thoughts or plans, immediately ***tell someone*** in that person's family or yours, other adults, or call 911, the operator, the police, a suicide hotline, or whatever number your area uses for emergency assistance.
- Remember, it is better to break a confidence and save a life, than to keep a secret. ***Secrets kill!***
- If you have suicidal thoughts, ***tell someone*** you know will help you: a family member, other adult, counselor, teacher, coach, spiritual advisor.
- If you trust no one, or if you know no one, then dial 911, the operator, the police, a suicide hotline, or whatever number your area uses for emergency assistance.

Risk Factors of Suicide

- Alcohol and other substance use disorders
- Feeling of hopelessness
- Impulsive and/or aggressive behavior
- Mental disorders, such as depression
- Personality changes
- History of trauma or abuse
- Previous suicide attempt
- Family history of suicide
- Job or financial problems
- Trouble studying and/or trouble with grades in school
- Changes in relationships and/or losses of relationships
- Lack of social support
- Sense of isolation or abandonment
- Shame associated with seeking help
- Barriers to accessing health care, especially mental health and substance abuse treatment
- Difficult times at home and/or school
- Cultural and religious beliefs that glorify suicide
- Influence of others who have died by suicide
- Ridicule and/or exclusion in response to a different religious belief, unique cultural dress or celebration, sexual preference or gender identity
- Easy access to effective ways to die by suicide
- Local events of suicide that spread a contagious influence

Warning Signs of Suicide

- Thinking or talking about suicide
- Substance use
- No sense of purpose or belonging
- Anger
- Feeling as if there is no way out
- Feeling as if there is nothing to live for
- Withdrawing from friends, family, schoolwork, sports, and school and social activities
- Anxious, nervous
- Isolating oneself
- High risk-taking behavior
- Unpredictable, sudden, baseless changes in mood
- Preoccupation with death
- Suddenly happier, calmer
- Sense of seeming distant
- Loss of interest in surroundings, activities and friends
- Little to no interest in school or school work
- Visiting or calling people one cares about but hasn't seen for a while
- Giving things away, especially prized possessions

Symptoms of Depression

The following symptoms are normal from time to time and arise for a variety of reasons, but experiencing several or more for more than two or three weeks may indicate the presence of depression or another mental illness. Check the symptoms that you believe a friend is currently experiencing, or check those that you are currently experiencing.

If you are answering for a friend, what is the person's name code? _____

- ❑ I cry or feel like crying a lot
- ❑ I am sad
- ❑ I am getting lower grades in school
- ❑ I'm bored
- ❑ I feel alone
- ❑ I feel empty
- ❑ I don't have confidence in myself anymore
- ❑ I often feel scared, but I don't know why
- ❑ I often feel angry
- ❑ I feel guilty
- ❑ I can't concentrate
- ❑ I have a hard time remembering things
- ❑ I have a hard time making decisions
- ❑ I feel like I'm in a fog
- ❑ I'm very tired, no matter how much I sleep
- ❑ I'm frustrated with everything and everybody
- ❑ I don't have fun anymore
- ❑ I feel helpless
- ❑ I'm always getting into trouble
- ❑ I'm restless and jittery and can't sit still
- ❑ I feel anxious
- ❑ I feel disorganized, as if my head is spinning.
- ❑ I feel self-conscious
- ❑ I feel that nobody cares about me
- ❑ I feel ugly
- ❑ I don't care about what I wear
- ❑ I'm too fat/thin/short/tall
- ❑ My body is not shapely enough
- ❑ I'll never make the team/choir
- ❑ I am, or I feel like, hurting myself
- ❑ I don't feel like talking anymore - I have nothing to say
- ❑ I feel my life has no direction
- ❑ I am consuming alcohol/drugs regularly
- ❑ My whole body feels slowed down
- ❑ I don't want to go out with my friends anymore
- ❑ I don't worry about my personal hygiene or appearance anymore
- ❑ My heart sometimes pounds and I can't catch my breath
- ❑ Sometimes I feel like I'm losing it
- ❑ I feel "different" from everyone else
- ❑ I smile, but inside I'm miserable
- ❑ I feel that life isn't worth living
- ❑ I have a hard time falling asleep
- ❑ I wake up and can't get back to sleep
- ❑ I have no appetite
- ❑ My appetite has increased – I eat all the time
- ❑ My weight has increased or decreased
- ❑ I have thoughts of suicide
- ❑ I have headaches, stomachaches and/or neck aches
- ❑ My arms and legs hurt
- ❑ I feel nauseous and/or dizzy
- ❑ I can't think straight
- ❑ Sometimes my vision seems blurred or slow
- ❑ I'm clumsy and feel off-balance
- ❑ Everyone hates me

If you have checked off several, it is time for you to talk to a trusted adult who can help you find a medical professional for yourself, or for the friend you had in mind.

Something to Think About

Write about why you think a person might want to consider suicide (a permanent solution) to a difficult time (temporary problem) in life.

What Can You Do?

If you, or people you know, are feeling depressed or suicidal, how can you use your voice?

Whole Person Associates is the leading publisher of training resources for professionals who empower people to create and maintain healthy lifestyles. Our creative resources will help you work effectively with your clients in the areas of stress management, wellness promotion, mental health and life skills.

Please visit us at our web site: **www.wholeperson.com**. You can check out our entire line of products, place an order, request our print catalog, and sign up for our monthly special notifications.

Whole Person Associates

800-247-6789